Storybook Cross-Stitch

by The Vanessa-Ann Collection

Storybook Cross-Stitch

by The Vanessa-Ann Collection

Meredith® Press
New York, New York

Meredith® Press is an imprint of Meredith® Books:
President, Book Group: Joseph J. Ward
Vice President, Editorial Director: Elizabeth P. Rice
For Meredith® Press:
Executive Editor: Maryanne Bannon
Senior Editor: Carol Spier
Associate Editor: Ruth Weadock
Production Manager: Bill Rose

For Chapelle Ltd.:
Owner: Jo Packham
Staff: Sandra Anderson, Malissa Boatwright, Trice Boerens, Rebecca Christensen, Holly Fuller,
Cherie Hanson, Holly Hollingsworth, Susan Jorgensen, Susan Laws, Amanda McPeck,
Tammy Perkins, Jamie Pierce, Leslie Ridenour, Edie Stockstill, Amy Vineyard,
Nancy Whitley, and Lorrie Young

Photographers: Ryne Hazen, Kevin Dilley
Framing: Artist's Touch

ISBN: 0-696-02385-7 (hardcover)
ISBN: 0-696-20436-3 (softcover)
Library of Congress Catalog Card Number: 93-086665
First Printing 1995

Distributed by Meredith Corporation, Des Moines, IA
10 9 8 7 6 5 4 3 2 1
Printed in the United States of America.

Dear Crafter,

Storybook Cross-Stitch is filled with fantastical images and faraway lands, memorable characters and lasting messages. Whether it's Androcles' kindness to the lion or Cinderella's happily-ever-after ending, these stories and poems are an integral part of childhood "quiet times," fond memories in the making for our grown-up years. Here, they are captured in cross-stitch forever, in designs both beautiful and whimsical, appealing to young and old alike.

Whichever projects you choose for displaying at home or giving as wonderful hand-crafted gifts, we've provided full-color photographs, easy-to-read color charts, and complete step-by-step directions for each piece. There are even helpful sewing and stitching Basics sections for your reference, plus a handy Suppliers list for materials and tools.

We hope you enjoy creating these delightful keepsakes as much as we enjoyed bringing them to you.

Sincerely,

Ruth Weadock
Associate Editor

Introduction

The nursery rhymes, fairy tails and fables you cherished as a child have been the favorites of both parents and children for hundreds of years. Countless readings of these timeless tales have bonded generations together as young ones sit on laps memorizing verses, giggling at the character voices, and discussing "the moral of the story."

Now you can pass on a token of these treasured moments with twenty-five beautiful designs by the artists of the Vanessa-Ann Collection. Each captures the magic of those special memories with the heirloom quality and personal touch only achieved in cross-stitch. These finished pieces will be keepsakes which, like the stories that inspired them, will be shared by future generations.

Jo Packham
Owner, The Vanessa-Ann Collection

Contents

Fairy

Rapunzel

The Frog Prince

Cinderella

Tales

Little Red Riding Hood

The Princess and the Pea

Rumpelstiltskin

Goldilocks and The Three Bears

Hansel and Gretel

Little Red Ridinghood

Little Red Ridinghood

LITTLE RED RIDING HOOD

... The Wolf walked with Little Red Ridinghood for a time, then said, "Look at the pretty roses! It is such a lovely day, I'm sure your grandmother would be pleased if you spent some time to gather some for her."

Little Red Ridinghood thought, "It is still early in the morning. I will have plenty of time to pick them." So she left the path and wandered deeper into the woods to pick flowers.

In the meantime the Wolf left her and ran straight off to her grandmother's cottage ...

Little Red Ridinghood

SAMPLE

Stitched on Sand Belfast Linen 32 over two threads, the finished design size is 6⅜" x 9¼". The fabric was cut 13" x 16". Frame as desired.

Other Fabrics	Finished Design
Aida 11	9¼" x 13⅜"
Aida 14	7¼" x 10½"
Aida 18	5⅝" x 8⅛"
Hardanger 22	4⅝" x 6⅝"

Anchor			DMC (used for sample)	
Step 1: Cross-stitch (2 strands)				
366	·		951	Peach Pecan-lt.
306	–		725	Topaz
9	▽		760	Salmon
11			350	Coral-med.
19			817	Coral Red-vy. dk.
118	△		340	Blue Violet-med.
101			327	Antique Violet-vy. dk.
145	○		334	Baby Blue-med.
149	●		336	Navy Blue
186	✕		959	Seagreen-med.
208	□		563	Jade-lt.
242	+		989	Forest Green
212	■		561	Jade-vy. dk.
379			840	Beige Brown-med.
380	▲		839	Beige Brown-dk.

Step 2: Backstitch (1 strand)

149		336	Navy Blue (Flowers, lettering)
382		3371	Black Brown (All else)

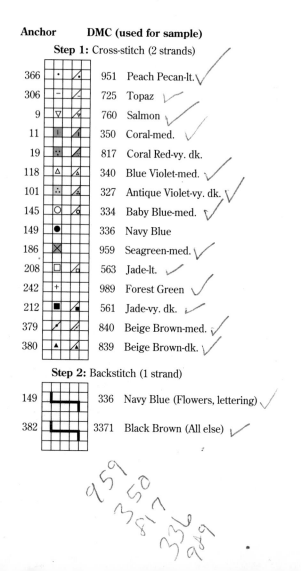

e Red Ridinghood

. . . One day, after the bears had made porridge for their breakfast, they walked out into the woods while the porridge was cooling. While they were walking, a little girl named Goldilocks came to the house. She peeped in the keyhole and then looked in the window where she saw the porridge. If she had been a thoughtful little girl, she might have waited until the bears returned, and perhaps they would have invited her to breakfast. But the porridge was tempting, and she opened the door so she could help herself . . .

The Story of the Three Bears

Goldilocks and

The Three Bears

Goldilocks and the Three Bears

SAMPLE
Stitched on Cream Murano 30 over two threads, the finished design size is 7⅝" x 10¼". The fabric was cut 13" x 16". Frame as desired.

Other Fabrics	Finished Design
Aida 11	10⅜" x 14"
Aida 14	8⅛" x 11"
Aida 18	6⅜" x 8½"
Hardanger 22	5⅛" x 7"

Anchor			DMC	(used for sample)

Step 1: Cross-stitch (2 strands)

Anchor			DMC	Name
1	+	.		White
387	△	△	712	Cream
306	·	·	725	Topaz ✓
307	I	/	977	Golden Brown-lt. ✓
8	—	/	761	Salmon-lt. ✓
42	O	6	3350	Dusty Rose-dk. ✓
104	·		210	Lavender-med. ✓
101	⊠	◿	327	Antique Violet-vy. dk. ✓
158	∴	◿	747	Sky Blue-vy. lt. ✓
167	▲	◢	519	Sky Blue ✓
168	⊠	◿	807	Peacock Blue ✓
840	△	◿	3768	Slate Green-dk. ✓
206	—	/	955	Nile Green-lt. ✓
216	□	◿	367	Pistachio Green-dk. ✓
882	·	◿	407	Pecan ✓
936	●	6	632	Pecan-dk. ✓
379	O	6	840	Beige Brown-med. ✓
380	⊠	◿	839	Beige Brown-dk. ✓
236		◢	3799	Pewter Gray-vy. dk.

Step 2: Backstitch (1 strand)

236		3799	Pewter Gray-vy. dk.

Step 3: French Knot (1 strand)

236	●	3799	Pewter Gray-vy. dk.

Top left • Stitch Count: 114 x 154

Bottom left

Bottom right

21

. . . They searched but they found no crumbs, for the birds had eaten them all. But a snow-white bird led them to a cottage made of gingerbread which was covered with candy and cakes. By this time, Hansel and Gretel were quite hungry.

"We can have a real feast now," said Hansel, not knowing of the evil witch who lurked inside . . .

Hansel
and
Gretel

Hansel and Gretel

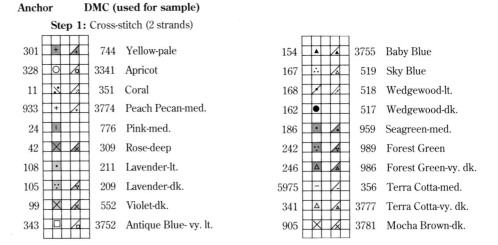

Anchor DMC (used for sample)

Step 1: Cross-stitch (2 strands)

Anchor			DMC	
301			744	Yellow-pale
328			3341	Apricot
11			351	Coral
933			3774	Peach Pecan-med.
24			776	Pink-med.
42			309	Rose-deep
108			211	Lavender-lt.
105			209	Lavender-dk.
99			552	Violet-dk.
343			3752	Antique Blue- vy. lt.
154			3755	Baby Blue
167			519	Sky Blue
168			518	Wedgewood-lt.
162			517	Wedgewood-dk.
186			959	Seagreen-med.
242			989	Forest Green
246			986	Forest Green-vy. dk.
5975			356	Terra Cotta-med.
341			3777	Terra Cotta-vy. dk.
905			3781	Mocha Brown-dk.

SAMPLE

Stitched on Antique White Murano 30 over two threads, the finished design size is 9¾" x 7⅞". The fabric was cut 16" x 14". Frame as desired.

Other Fabrics	Finished Design
Aida 11	13⅜" x 10⅞"
Aida 14	10½" x 8½"
Aida 18	8⅛" x 6⅝"
Hardanger 22	6⅝" x 5⅜"

Top left • Stitch Count: 147 x 119

127 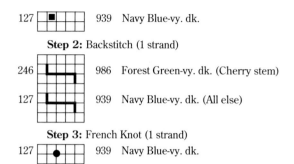 939   Navy Blue-vy. dk.

Step 2: Backstitch (1 strand)

246   986   Forest Green-vy. dk. (Cherry stem)

127   939   Navy Blue-vy. dk. (All else)

Step 3: French Knot (1 strand)

127   939   Navy Blue-vy. dk.

Hansel and Gretel

Bottom left

26

At my house?

Bottom right

The Frog Prince

THE FROG PRINCE

"You see, I wasn't what I seemed to be," he said. "An evil woman cast a spell on me that no one but you could break."

She could say nothing as she gazed at the boy prince who had been a large, ugly frog only moments earlier.

"Will you let me be your playmate now?" he asked.

The Princess laughed, and they ran outside together to play with her gold ball, now as the best of friends.

The Frog Prince

SAMPLE

Stitched on Platinum Belfast Linen 32 over two
threads, the finished design size is 10" x 7".
The fabric was cut 17" x 13". Frame as desired.

Other Fabrics	Finished Design
Aida 11	14⅝" x 10⅛"
Aida 14	11½" x 8"
Aida 18	9" x 6¼"
Hardanger 22	7⅜" x 5⅛"

The color key is found on page 32.

31

The Frog Prince

Anchor   DMC (used for sample)

Step 1: Cross-stitch (2 strands)

Anchor			DMC	
293			727	Topaz-vy. lt.
306			725	Topaz
366			951	Peach Pecan-lt.
881			945	Peach Beige
48			818	Baby Pink
74			3354	Dusty Rose-vy. lt.
76			3731	Dusty Rose-med.
95			554	Violet-lt.
99			552	Violet-dk.
159			3325	Baby Blue-lt.
168			518	Wedgewood-lt.
162			517	Wedgewood-dk.
264			772	Pine Green-lt.
203			564	Jade-vy. lt.
843			3364	Pine Green
861			3363	Pine Green-med.
376			842	Beige Brown-vy. lt.
882			3773	Pecan-vy. lt.
379			840	Beige Brown-med.
309			435	Brown-vy. lt.
351			400	Mahogany-dk.
381			838	Beige Brown-vy. dk.
8581			647	Beaver Gray-med.
273			3787	Brown Gray-dk.
403			310	Black

Step 2: Backstitch (1 strand)

306		725	Topaz (Roses)
403		310	Black (All else)

Step 3: Beads

●	62012	Royal Plumb

Top left

The Princess

. . . The Queen laid twenty mattresses on top of the pea and twenty quilts on top of the mattresses.

"Now we shall see if she is a true princess," she told the king.

The next morning the Queen asked the Princess how she had slept.

"Very badly," she replied. "I slept on something so hard my whole body is black and blue."

Then they knew she was a true princess as she had claimed . . .

and the Pea

The Princess and the Pea

SAMPLE

Stitched on Delicate Teal Jobelan 28 over two threads, the finished design size is 5⅞" x 11¼". The fabric was cut 13" x 18". As shown, pillow measures 21" x 14".

Other Fabrics	Finished Design
Aida 11	7½" x 14¼"
Aida 14	5⅞" x 11¼"
Aida 18	4⅝" x 8¾"
Hardanger 22	3¾" x 7⅛"

The color key is found on page 38.

Pillow Materials

- ½ yard of light pink fabric
- 1 yard of light blue printed fabric
- ⅛ yard of teal fabric
- ½ yard of periwinkle fabric for piping
- ½ yard of paper-backed fusible web
- Matching thread
- Polyester stuffing
- 1 yard of ¼"-diameter cable cord for piping
- 2 yards of ⅜"-diameter cable cord for piping
- Small green button

Pillow Directions

All seams ½" except where noted.

1. Referring to photo for placement, sew button onto stitched piece. With completed design centered, trim stitched piece to 9½" x 14½". From periwinkle fabric, make 1 yard of ¼"-diameter piping (see General Instructions on bias strips and piping). Cut into two 15" pieces. Sew strips to each long side of completed cross-stitch.

2. Cut two pieces of print fabric 28" x 4½". Gather both long edges of each piece until each is 14" long. Cut two 14½" x 2½" pieces each of light pink and teal fabric. Sew one of each color to opposite long edges of each gathered piece. Sew light pink edges to long sides of completed cross-stitch.

3. Cut a 20" x 14½" piece of fusible web. Fuse to wrong side of pillow front following manufacturer's instructions.

4. From periwinkle fabric, make 2 yards of ⅜"-diameter piping. Sew to front of pillow.

5. From light pink fabric, cut a 22" x 15" piece for pillow back. Sew to pillow front (see General Instructions on finishing pillows). Turn right side out; stuff; slipstitch closed.

Top left • Stitch Count: 83 x 157

The Princess and the Pea

Anchor   DMC (used for sample)

Step 1: Cross-stitch (2 strands)

Anchor		DMC	
1	△		White
306		725	Topaz
48	I	818	Baby Pink
893	●	224	Shell Pink-lt.
10	▲	352	Coral-lt.
11	·	3328	Salmon-dk.
42	–	335	Rose
59	◯	326	Rose-vy. dk.
118	□	340	Blue Violet-med.
119	■	333	Blue Violet-dk.
185	✕	964	Seagreen-lt.
154	◯	3755	Baby Blue
978	✕	322	Navy Blue-vy. lt.
878	△	501	Blue Green-dk.
885	·	739	Tan-ultra vy. lt.
882	I	407	Pecan
936		632	Pecan-dk.
382	+	3021	Brown Gray-vy. dk.

Step 2: Backstitch (1 strand)

382		3021	Brown Gray-vy. dk.

Bottom left

Bottom right

Cinderella

. . . He asked Cinderella to sit. Putting the slipper to her foot, he was astonished to find it went on easily. The surprise of her sisters was great, but was still greater when Cinderella pulled out of her pocket the second slipper.

The Prince courted Cinderella for a few days afterward and found her even more charming than before. Soon they were married, and they lived happily ever after . . .

Cinderella

SAMPLE
Stitched on White Murano 30 over two threads, the finished design size is 9½" x 8¼". The fabric was cut 16" x 15". Frame as desired.

Other Fabrics	Finished Design
Aida 11	12⅞" x 11¼"
Aida 14	10⅛" x 8⅞"
Aida 18	7⅞" x 6⅞"
Hardanger 22	6½" x 5⅝"

Anchor			DMC (used for sample)	
		Step 1: Cross-stitch (2 strands)		
386	i	⁄	746	Off White
366	+	⁄	951	Peach Pecan-lt.
891	X	⁄	676	Old Gold-lt.
323	·	⁄	722	Orange Spice-lt.
326	∴	⁄	720	Orange Spice-dk.
892	□	⁄	225	Shell Pink-vy. lt.
893	◇	⁄	224	Shell Pink-lt.
74	○	⁄	3354	Dusty Rose-vy. lt.
69	▦	⁄	3687	Mauve

Top left • Stitch Count: 142 x 124

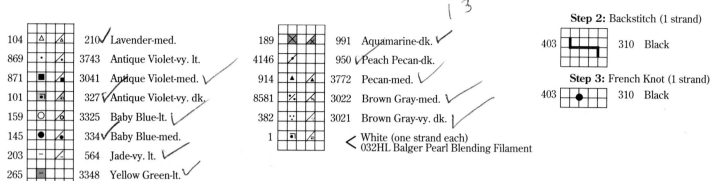

104	△	⟋	210	Lavender-med.
869	·	⟋	3743	Antique Violet-vy. lt.
871	■	◣	3041	Antique Violet-med.
101	⊡	⟋	327	Antique Violet-vy. dk.
159	○	⟋	3325	Baby Blue-lt.
145	●	⟋	334	Baby Blue-med.
203	−		564	Jade-vy. lt.
265	▬		3348	Yellow Green-lt.
186	▽	⟋	993	Aquamarine-lt.

189	⊠	⟋	991	Aquamarine-dk.
4146	⟋		950	Peach Pecan-dk.
914	▲	⟋	3772	Pecan-med.
8581	⧄		3022	Brown Gray-med.
382	⁝		3021	Brown Gray-vy. dk.
1	⊡	⟋	< White (one strand each) 032HL Balger Pearl Blending Filament

Step 2: Backstitch (1 strand)

| 403 | ⌐ | 310 | Black |

Step 3: French Knot (1 strand)

| 403 | ● | 310 | Black |

Top right

43

Cinderella

Rapunzel

. . . The Prince had heard
Rapunzel's voice, but searched
in vain for a door to the
tower. Then one day, as he hid
behind a tree, he heard the
Witch call out:

Rapunzel, Rapunzel, let
down your golden hair.

"So that is the way up,"
the Prince said. "Then I will
climb up, too, and visit the
maiden . . ."

Rapunzel

SAMPLE

Stitched on Pewter Murano 30 over two
threads, the finished design size is 6½" x 8⅜".
The fabric was cut 13" x 15".

Other Fabrics	Finished Design
Aida 11	8⅞" x 11⅜"
Aida 14	6⅞" x 8⅞"
Aida 18	5⅜" x 7
Hardanger 22	4⅜" x 5⅝"

Tray

The tray shown is made from a picture frame
with a mat, glass, sturdy backing, and handles.
The mat opening is about 7" x 8¾". For best
results, have it framed by a professional framer.

Anchor	DMC (used for sample)	

Step 1: Cross-stitch (2 strands)

1		White
301	744	Yellow-pale
891	676	Old Gold-lt.
4146	754	Peach-lt.
9	760	Salmon
75	3733	Dusty Rose-lt.
42	309	Rose-deep
104	210	Lavender-med.
101	327	Antique Violet-vy. dk.
119	333	Blue Violet-dk.
167	519	Sky Blue
978	322	Navy Blue-vy. lt.
816	3750	Antique Blue-vy. dk.
208	563	Jade-lt.
242	989	Forest Green
363	436	Tan
397	762	Pearl Gray-vy. lt.
398	415	Pearl Gray
400	414	Steel Gray-dk.
401	317	Pewter Gray

Step 2: Backstitch (1 strand)

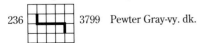

| 236 | 3799 | Pewter Gray-vy. dk. |

Top left • Stitch Count: 97 x 125

Rapunzel

Bottom left

50

The Magic Word

RUMPLESTILTSKIN!

Rumplestiltskin

. . . The little man was certain the Queen could never guess his name, and the child would become his!

"Is your name Conrad?"

"No," he answered.

"Is it Harry?"

"It is not!" he cackled.

Then with a gleam in her eye, the Queen asked, "Would your name, perhaps, be Rumplestiltskin?"

Rumplestiltskin

SAMPLE

Stitched on White Murano 30 over two threads, the finished design size is 5⅝" x 7⅜". The fabric was cut 17" x 17". As shown, pillow measures 20" x 20" including ruffle.

Other Fabrics	Finished Design
Aida 11	7¾" x 10¾"
Aida 14	6⅛" x 8⅜"
Aida 18	4¾" x 6½"
Hardanger 22	3⅞" x 5⅜"

The color key is found on page 56.

Pillow Materials

- 7¾ yards of 2½"–wide white eyelet
- Three white buttons (four holes)
- Three pink buttons (four holes)
- Green, white, and pink embroidery floss for buttons
- 1½ yards of 54"–wide pink print fabric
- 1 yard of ½"–wide lace trim
- 1½" yard of ½"–diameter cable cord for piping
- Matching thread
- #100/16 sewing machine needle
- Polyester stuffing

Large French knots: two strands, three wraps. Use pink floss for white buttons, white floss for pink buttons

Long stitches with green floss: four strands

Button Diagram

Pillow Directions

All seams ½".

1. With completed design centered, cut piece 14" x 14". Cut 2½"–wide eyelet into four 14" strips. With right sides up and straight edges even, pin a length of eyelet to each edge of completed cross-stitch. Fold miters at corners, trim to ½" seam allowance and slip-stitch. Baste in place. Tack down points of eyelet.

2. From ½"–wide trim, cut two pieces 6⅝" long and two pieces 8⅜" long. Sew to completed cross-stitch, forming a lace border ½" beyond design border.

3. Referring to Button Diagram (left), sew buttons to sides of piece as shown in photo.

4. From pink print fabric, cut a 14" square and four 8" x 54" pieces; set aside. From remainder of fabric, make 1¼ yards of ½"–diameter corded piping; sew to pillow front (see General Instructions on bias strips and piping). Attach corded piping to perimeter of finished piece.

5. Sew all short ends of 8" x 54" pieces together to make a complete circle. Then press in half, wrong sides together and raw edges aligned. Cut four 54"-long pieces of 2½"–wide eyelet; sew together in same manner. Lay eyelet on top of fabric, straight edges aligned. Treating all three layers as one, gather each 54" section of the circle to 14". Pin to completed cross-stitch with right sides together, raw edges aligned, and seams at corners. Sew together.

6. Referring to General Instructions on finishing pillows, sew remaining 14" square to stitched piece. Turn right side out; stuff; slipstitch closed.

Top right

55

Rumplestiltskin

Anchor			DMC (used for sample)
Step 1: Cross-stitch (2 strands)			
926	+	⁄	Ecru
366	·	⁄	951 Peach Pecan-lt.
293	✕	⁄	727 Topaz-vy. lt.
890	●	⁄	729 Old Gold-med.
49	·	⁄	3689 Mauve-lt.
66	◯	⁄	3688 Mauve-med.
158	−	⁄	775 Baby Blue-vy. lt.
159	✕	⁄	3325 Baby Blue-lt.
978	△	⁄	322 Navy Blue-vy. lt.
928	⁄	⁄	598 Turquoise-lt.
167	✕	⁄	597 Turquoise
208	−	⁄	563 Jade-lt.
210	☐	⁄	562 Jade-med.
5968	◯	⁄	355 Terra Cotta-dk.
378	¦	⁄	841 Beige Brown-lt.
401	∴	⁄	413 Pewter Gray-dk.
403	▲	⁄	310 Black
Step 2: Backstitch (1 strand)			
403			310 Black
Step 3: French Knot (1 strand)			
403	●		310 Black

Bottom left

56

Nursery

The Old Woman who Lived in a Shoe

Ring A Ring O Roses

Rock-a-Bye Baby

Twinkle, Twinkle, Little Star

Rhymes

Little Bo Peep

Mary, Mary, Quite Contrary

Jack Sprat

Hey Diddle Diddle, the Cat and the Fiddle

Hey diddle, diddle,
  The cat and the fiddle,
The cow jumped
  Over the moon.

The little dog laughed,
  To see such a sport,
And the dish ran away
  With the spoon.

...The Cow Jumped
Over the Moon

Hey Diddle Diddle,
The Cat and the Fiddle . . .

SAMPLE
Stitched on Delicate Teal Jobelan 28 over two threads, the finished design size is 5⅝" x 8⅝". The fabric was cut 12" x 15". Frame as desired.

Other Fabrics	Finished Design
Aida 11	7⅛" x 10⅞"
Aida 14	5⅝" x 8⅝"
Aida 18	4⅜" x 6⅝"
Hardanger 22	3½" x 5½"

Anchor			DMC (used for sample)
Step 1: Cross-stitch (2 strands)			
926			Ecru
66			3688 Mauve-med.
69			3687 Mauve
104			210 Lavender-med.
110			208 Lavender-vy. dk.
167			597 Turquoise
189			991 Aquamarine-dk.
886			3047 Yellow Beige-lt.
373			3045 Yellow Beige-dk.
363			436 Tan
371			433 Brown-med.
382			3371 Black Brown

Step 2: Backstitch (1 strand)

382		3371 Black Brown

Top • Stitch Count: 78 x 120

... The Cow Jumped Over the Moon

Other Fabrics	Finished Design
Aida 11	6⅞" x 11⅞"
Aida 14	5½" x 9⅜"
Aida 18	4¼" x 7¼"
Hardanger 22	3½" x 6"

Anchor		DMC (used for sample)	

Step 1: Cross-stitch (2 strands)

1			White
881		945	Peach Beige
293		727	Topaz-vy. lt.
306		725	Topaz
74		3354	Dusty Rose-vy. lt.
101		327	Antique Violet-vy. dk.
158		775	Baby Blue-vy. lt.
121		794	Cornflower Blue-lt.
928		598	Turquoise-lt.
167		597	Turquoise
208		563	Jade-lt.
843		3364	Pine Green
257		3346	Hunter Green
885		739	Tan-ultra vy. lt.
370		434	Brown-lt.
397		3072	Beaver Gray-vy. lt.
236		3799	Pewter Gray-vy. dk.

Step 2: Backstitch (1 strand)

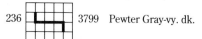

| 236 | | 3799 | Pewter Gray-vy. dk. |

Step 3: French Knot (1 strand)

| 236 | | 3799 | Pewter Gray-vy. dk. |

Top • Stitch Count: 76 x 131

Ring A Ring

Ring a ring o roses,
    A pocket full of posies.
Ashes, ashes,
    We all fall down!

O Roses

Ring A Ring O Roses

SAMPLE

Stitched on Light Mocha Belfast Linen 32
over two threads, the finished design size is
10" x 8½". The fabric was cut 16" x 15".
Frame as desired.

Other Fabrics	Finished Design
Aida 11	14½" x 12⅜"
Aida 14	11⅜" x 9¾"
Aida 18	8⅞" x 7½"
Hardanger 22	7¼" x 6⅛"

Anchor		DMC (used for sample)
	Step 1: Cross-stitch (2 strands)	
1		White
293		727 Topaz-vy. lt.
295		726 Topaz-lt.
306		725 Topaz
891		676 Old Gold-lt.
307		783 Christmas Gold
892		3770 Peach Pecan-vy. lt.
893		819 Baby Pink-lt.
48		818 Baby Pink
24		776 Pink-med.

Top left • Stitch Count: 160 x 136

25	3326	Rose-lt.
27	899	Rose-med.
42	335	Rose
59	309	Rose-deep
47	321	Christmas Red
46	666	Christmas Red-bright
20	498	Christmas Red-dk.
43	815	Garnet-med.
264	472	Avocado Green-ultra lt.
266	471	Avocado Green-vy. lt.

255	907	Parrot Green-lt.
256	906	Parrot Green-med.
257	905	Parrot Green-dk.
258	904	Parrot Green-vy. dk.
238	703	Chartreuse
227	701	Christmas Green-lt.
862	520	Fern Green-dk.
868	758	Terra Cotta-lt.
337	3778	Terra Cotta
5975	356	Terra Cotta-med.

5968	355	Terra Cotta-dk.
370	434	Brown-lt.
905	3031	Mocha Brown-vy. dk.
387	822	Beige Gray-lt.
830	644	Beige Gray-med.
397	762	Pearl Gray-vy. lt.
399	318	Steel Gray-lt.

Step 2: Backstitch (1 strand)

| 905 | 3031 | Mocha Brown-vy. dk. |

Bottom left

Ring A Ring O Roses

Top right

Rock-a-Bye Baby

Rock-a-bye baby
On the tree top,
When the wind blows
The cradle will rock.

When the bough breaks
The cradle will fall,
And down will come baby
Cradle and all.

Rock-a-bye
Baby

Mary Elizabeth
Grey
JUNE 1, 1900

Rock-a-Bye Baby

SAMPLE
Stitched on Cream Murano 30 over two threads, the finished design size is 7¾" x 10¼". The fabric was cut 14" x 17". Frame as desired.

Other Fabrics	Finished Design
Aida 11	10⅝" x 13⅞"
Aida 14	8⅜" x 10⅞"
Aida 18	6½" x 8½"
Hardanger 22	5⅜" x 7"

A child's name and birth date may be centered on a 14" x 6" piece of Cream Murano 30 over two threads, and framed below the cross-stitch piece. Use an alphabet found on pages 80 or 81.

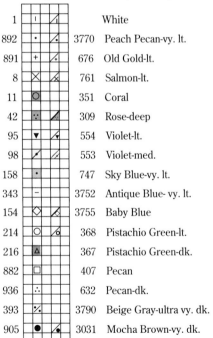

Anchor		DMC (used for sample)	
Step 1: Cross-stitch (2 strands)			
1			White
892		3770	Peach Pecan-vy. lt.
891		676	Old Gold-lt.
8		761	Salmon-lt.
11		351	Coral
42		309	Rose-deep
95		554	Violet-lt.
98		553	Violet-med.
158		747	Sky Blue-vy. lt.
343		3752	Antique Blue- vy. lt.
154		3755	Baby Blue
214		368	Pistachio Green-lt.
216		367	Pistachio Green-dk.
882		407	Pecan
936		632	Pecan-dk.
393		3790	Beige Gray-ultra vy. dk.
905		3031	Mocha Brown-vy. dk.

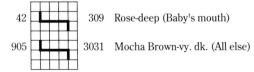

Step 2: Backstitch (1 strand)			
42		309	Rose-deep (Baby's mouth)
905		3031	Mocha Brown-vy. dk. (All else)

Top left • Stitch Count: 117 x 153

Bottom left

81

Jack Sprat
     Could eat no fat,
His wife
     Could eat no lean.
And so between
     The two of them,
They licked the
     Platter clean.

Jack Sprat

Jack Sprat

SAMPLE

Stitched on Antique White Belfast Linen 32 over two threads, the finished design size is 5⅛" x 5¾". The fabric was cut 12" x 12". Frame as desired.

Other Fabrics	Finished Design
Aida 11	7½" x 8¼"
Aida 14	5⅞" x 6½"
Aida 18	4½" x 5"
Hardanger 22	3¾" x 4⅛"

Anchor   DMC (used for sample)

Step 1: Cross-stitch (2 strands)

Anchor		DMC	
1			White
4146		754	Peach-lt.
868		758	Terra Cotta-lt.
9		760	Salmon
48		818	Baby Pink
24		776	Pink-med.
27		893	Carnation-lt.
42		309	Rose-deep
108		211	Lavender-lt.
86		3608	Plum-vy. lt.
87		3607	Plum-lt.
121		793	Cornflower Blue-med.
940		792	Cornflower Blue-dk.
206		955	Nile Green-lt.
203		954	Nile Green
204		912	Emerald Green-lt.
228		910	Emerald Green-dk.
891 / 307		676 / 977	Old Gold-lt. (1 strand) / Golden Brown-lt. (1 strand)
307		977	Golden Brown-lt.
308		976	Golden Brown-med.
355		975	Golden Brown-dk.
379		840	Beige Brown-med.
380		839	Beige Brown-dk.

Top left • Stitch Count: 82 x 91

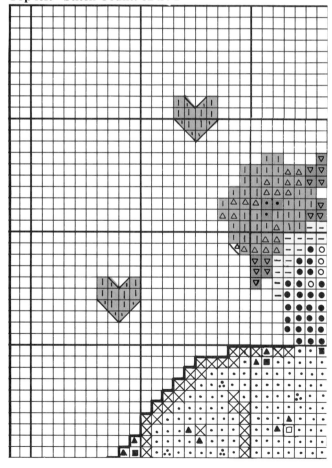

Step 2: Backstitch (1 strand)

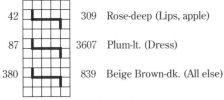

42	309	Rose-deep (Lips, apple)
87	3607	Plum-lt. (Dress)
380	839	Beige Brown-dk. (All else)

Step 3: French Knot (1 strand)

380	839	Beige Brown-dk.

Top right

Jack Sprat

Bottom left

86

Bottom right

Little Bo Peep

Little Bo Peep
　Has lost her sheep
And doesn't know where
　To find them.

Leave them alone
　And they'll come home,
Wagging their tails
　Behind them.

Little Bo Peep

SAMPLE

Stitched on White Belfast Linen 32 over two threads, the finished design size is 7¾" x 7½". The fabric was cut 14" x 14".

Other Fabrics	Finished Design
Aida 11	11⅛" x 10⅞"
Aida 14	8¾" x 8½"
Aida 18	6⅞" x 6⅝"
Hardanger 22	5⅝" x 5⅜"

Clock Materials

• Sudbury House Clock without face
• 8-ounce bottle of light green acrylic paint
• 8-ounce bottle of dark walnut antiquing glaze
• Paper towels
• Purchased small wooden sheep and trees
• Gray, dark gray, brown, white, green, and yellow acrylic paints
• Small sponge
• Medium and small paintbrushes
• 6" piece of ⅜" pink satin ribbon
• 18" piece of ⅛" pink satin ribbon
• Pink thread
• hot-glue gun with glue sticks

Clock Directions

1. Paint clock with one coat of light green paint. Let dry. Dip brush in antiquing glaze. Remove excess glaze from brush and dab on a paper towel. Lightly brush piece so that the glaze streaks, but does not completely cover piece. Remove portions of wet glaze with towel or rag if needed.

2. Paint tree trunk brown and leaves green; sponge over leaves with white paint as desired. Paint sheep gray; sponge with white, except for feet and faces. Add details to face, ears, and legs with dark gray paint, referring to photo. Let dry. Tie 9" pieces of ⅛" pink satin ribbon around necks of sheep; trim as desired.

Top left • Stitch Count: 123 x 119

3. Tie ⅜" pink satin ribbon into a bow; sew onto staff as shown in photo.

4. Insert completed cross-stitch piece and assemble clock following manufacturer's instructions. Paint flowers on front of glass using green and yellow paints as shown. Hot-glue small wooden pieces to clock.

Anchor   DMC (used for sample)

Step 1: Cross-stitch (2 strands)

Anchor		DMC	
1			White
306		725	Topaz
886		677	Old Gold-vy. lt.
891		676	Old Gold-lt.
890		729	Old Gold-med.

Anchor	DMC	
4146	754	Peach-lt.
868	758	Terra Cotta-lt.
24	776	Pink-med.
25	3326	Rose-lt.
27	899	Rose-med.
76	3731	Dusty Rose-med.
128	800	Delft-pale
130	809	Delft
121	793	Cornflower Blue-med.
242	989	Forest Green
338	3776	Mahogany-lt.
349	301	Mahogany-med.
352	300	Mahogany-vy. dk.
397	762	Pearl Gray-vy. lt.
398	415	Pearl Gray

Step 2: Long, loose stitch (2 strands)

306		725	Topaz (Laces in dress)

Step 3: Backstitch (1 strand)

400		414	Steel Gray-dk. (Clothes, sheep, numbers, shoes, bows)
352		300	Mahogany-vy. dk. (All else)

Top right

Little Bo Peep

Bottom left

Twinkle, Twinkle Little Star

Twinkle, twinkle little star,
How I wonder what you are.

Up above the world so high,
Like a diamond in the sky!

Twinkle, Twinkle Little Star

SAMPLE

Stitched on Ivory Murano 30 over two threads, the finished design size is 6⅛" x 6⅜". The fabric was cut 13" x 13".

Other Fabrics	Finished Design
Aida 11	8⅜" x 8⅝"
Aida 14	6⅝" x 6¾"
Aida 18	5⅛" x 5¼"
Hardanger 22	4⅛" x 4⅜"

The color key is found on page 98.

Box Materials

• Box with 6½" x 6½" insert (See suppliers, page 167)
• Small sponge
• Purple, blue, pink, and yellow acrylic paints
• 3" x 5" index card
• Small paintbrush
• Foamcore or heavy cardboard same size as opening on box top
• Straight pins, or hot-glue gun and glue sticks
• Small pieces of polyester batting
• Newspaper or paper towel

Box Directions

1. Dab a small sponge in purple, blue, or pink paint and blot excess paint onto newspaper or paper towel. When desired effect is achieved on paper, dab paint onto box. Repeat with remaining colors until entire box is covered with a pleasing blend. Allow to dry completely.

2. Cut a star stencil from index card. Randomly sponge-paint yellow stars through the stencil onto sides of box (or paint them hand with a small paintbrush).

ard to fit box top opening. Layer and vester batting on top of board to ss. Pin or hot-glue completed to underside of Foamcore or o box.

Top left • Stitch Count: 92 x 95

Twinkle, Twinkle Little Star

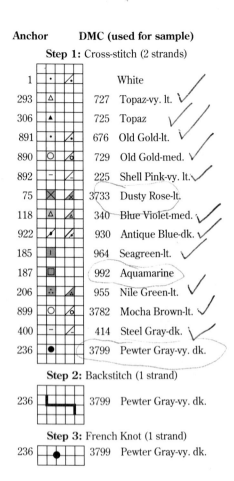

Anchor   **DMC (used for sample)**

Step 1: Cross-stitch (2 strands)

1				White
293			727	Topaz-vy. lt.
306			725	Topaz
891			676	Old Gold-lt.
890			729	Old Gold-med.
892			225	Shell Pink-vy. lt.
75			3733	Dusty Rose-lt.
118			340	Blue Violet-med.
922			930	Antique Blue-dk.
185			964	Seagreen-lt.
187			992	Aquamarine
206			955	Nile Green-lt.
899			3782	Mocha Brown-lt.
400			414	Steel Gray-dk.
236			3799	Pewter Gray-vy. dk.

Step 2: Backstitch (1 strand)

236   3799   Pewter Gray-vy. dk.

Step 3: French Knot (1 strand)

236   3799   Pewter Gray-vy. dk.

Bottom left

twinkle little star

Bottom right

Mary, Mary, Quite Contrary

Mary, Mary, quite contrary
How does your garden grow?

With silver bells and cockle shells
And pretty maids all in a row?

Mary, Mary, Quite Contrary

SAMPLE
Stitched on Cream Murano 30 over two
threads, the finished design size is
6¼" x 10½". The fabric was cut 13" x 17".
Frame as desired.

Other Fabrics	Finished Design
Aida 11	8½" x 14⅜"
Aida 14	6⅝" x 11¼"
Aida 18	5⅛" x 8¾"
Hardanger 22	4¼" x 7⅛"

Anchor		DMC (used for sample)	

Step 1: Cross-stitch (2 strands)

1	White
292	3078 Golden Yellow-vy. lt.
891	676 Old Gold-lt.
880	948 Peach-vy. lt.
4146	754 Peach-lt.
328	3341 Apricot
347	402 Mahogany-vy. lt.
324	922 Copper-lt.
69	3687 Mauve
95	554 Violet-lt.
343	3752 Antique Blue- vy. lt.
168	518 Wedgewood-lt.
206	955 Nile Green-lt.
268	3345 Hunter Green-dk.
371	433 Brown-med.
397	762 Pearl Gray-vy. lt.

Step 2: Backstitch (1 strand)

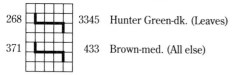

268	3345 Hunter Green-dk. (Leaves)
371	433 Brown-med. (All else)

Step 3: French Knot (1 strand)

371	433 Brown-med.

Top left • Stitch Count: 94 x 158

Mary, Mary, Quite Contrary

Bottom left

The Old Woman

Steven

Cass

Andrew

Katie

Lisa

Cole

Sara

Who Lived in a Shoe

Mark Alisa Justin Amy Beth Ann Billy Ryan

There was an old woman,
Who lived in a shoe.

She had so many children,
She didn't know what to do . . .

The Old Woman Who Lived in a Shoe

SAMPLE
Stitched on Cream Belfast Linen 32 over two threads, the finished design size is 9¼" x 7½". The fabric was cut 16" x 14".

Other Fabrics	Finished Design
Aida 11	13⅜" x 10⅞"
Aida 14	10½" x 8⅝"
Aida 18	8⅛" x 6⅝"
Hardanger 22	6⅝" x 5½"

Photo Album Materials

- Fabric-covered photo album
- Paper-backed fusible web
- ⅜"–wide ribbon: 1 yard, or enough to trim completed cross-stitch, including bow
- Fabric glue

Photo Album Directions

1. Cut fusible interfacing and completed cross-stitch piece to desired size (same size). Following manufacturer's instructions, fuse interfacing to wrong side of finished piece, then center and fuse piece to photo album.

2. Place midpoint of ribbon on upper left corner of cross-stitch. Fold ribbon to miter corner (see photo) and secure with glue. Continue gluing ribbon to perimeter of cross-stitch, mitering the corners, until ribbon meets in lower right corner. Tie ribbon in bow, and secure middle knot and ends of bow to album with glue.

Top left • Stitch Count: 147 x 120

Anchor   **DMC (used for sample)**

Step 1: Cross-stitch (2 strands)

Anchor			DMC	Name
1				White
301			744	Yellow-pale
891			676	Old Gold-lt.
4146			754	Peach-lt.
9			760	Salmon
24			776	Pink-med.
26			957	Geranium-pale
76			961	Wild Rose-dk.
11			350	Coral-med.
13			349	Coral-dk.
22			816	Garnet
99			552	Violet-dk.
101			550	Violet-vy. dk.
128			800	Delft-pale
130			799	Delft-med.
132			797	Royal Blue

Anchor			DMC	Name
264			772	Pine Green-lt.
242			989	Forest Green
246			986	Forest Green-vy. dk.
338			3776	Mahogany-lt.
349			301	Mahogany-med.
352			300	Mahogany-vy. dk.
360			898	Coffee Brown-vy. dk.
382			3371	Black Brown
397			762	Pearl Gray-vy. lt.

Step 2: Backstitch (1 strand)

			DMC	Name
338			3776	Mahogany-lt. (Daisies)
382			3371	Black Brown (All else)

Step 3: French Knot (1 strand)

			DMC	Name
382			3371	Black Brown

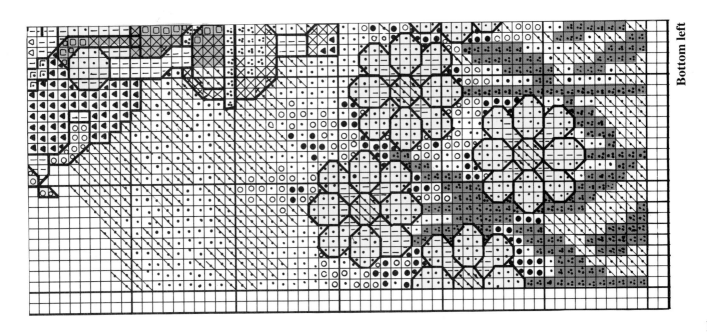

Bottom left

109

The Old Woman Who Lived in a Shoe

Top center

110

The Old Woman Who Lived in a Shoe

Top right

112

Bottom right

Fables

The Leopard and the Fox

The Wind and the Sun

The Wolf in Sheep's Clothing

Androcles and the Lion

The Goose that Laid the Golden Egg

The Tortoise and the Hare

The Fisherman and His Wife

The Country mouse and City m

The Goose that Laid

Once there was an old man who owned a special goose that could lay golden eggs. Every day he would take her one egg into town and exchange it for money. One day he said to himself, "This goose must be full of eggs. If I could get them all at once, I would have much more money." So the man killed the goose, but when he cut her open, there were no golden eggs inside. As a reward for his impatience and greed, he lost everything he had.

the Golden Egg

The Goose that Laid the Golden Egg

SAMPLE

Stitched on Sand Belfast Linen 32 over two threads, the finished design size is 5⅛" x 8½". The fabric was cut 15" x 19". As shown, pillow measures 11¼" x 15".

Other Fabrics	Finished Design
Aida 11	7½" x 12½"
Aida 14	5⅞" x 9¾"
Aida 18	4½" x 7⅝"
Hardanger 22	3¾" x 6¼"

Pillow Materials

- ½ yard of 45" paisley fabric
- 1⅝ yard of ½"-diameter green braided satin piping for edge
- 1⅛ yard of ⅛"-diameter gold piping
- Paper-backed fusible web
- Matching thread
- Polyester stuffing

Pillow Directions

All seams are ½".

1. From print fabric, cut two pieces 12" x 3" and two pieces 16" x 3". Sew pieces together to form a rectangular fabric frame, mitering the corners.

2. Referring to General Instructions on piping, sew gold piping to the inner edges of the fabric frame.

3. Cut four pieces of fusible web to same dimensions as fabric for Step 1. Following manufacturer's instructions, fuse to the wrong side of the frame. Remove paper; center and fuse frame to stitched piece. Trim edges even. Sew braided piping to perimeter.

4. Cut 12½" x 16½" rectangle from paisley fabric for backing. Referring to General Instructions on finishing pillows, sew back to front, turn right side out and stuff. Slipstitch closed.

Anchor			DMC	(used for sample)
			Step 1: Cross-stitch (2 strands)	
926	·	◿		Ecru
300	○	◿	745	Yellow-lt. pale
306	◢	◿	725	Topaz
881	△	◿	945	Peach Beige
868	ı	◿	3779	Terra Cotta-vy. lt.
10	⁒		3712	Salmon-med.
11	◿		3328	Salmon-dk.
76	◑	◢	3731	Dusty Rose-med.
42	⊠	◺	3350	Dusty Rose-dk.
970	▲	◿	315	Antique Mauve-vy. dk.
969	U		3727	Antique Mauve-lt.
108	+	◿	211	Lavender-lt.
105	·	◿	209	Lavender-dk.
117	□	◪	341	Blue Violet-lt.
928	△		598	Turquoise-lt.
206	–	◿	955	Nile Green-lt.
215	⠴	◿	320	Pistachio Green-med.
373	✕	◿	3045	Yellow Beige-dk.
903	⋂		3032	Mocha Brown-med.
393	■	◣	3790	Beige Gray-ultra vy. dk.
306	●	◿	725	Topaz 017HL Balger Blending Filament
			Step 2: Backstitch (1 strand)	
117			341	Blue Violet-lt. (Inside goose)
382			3021	Brown Gray-vy. dk. (All else)
			Step 3: French Knot (1 strand)	
382	●		3021	Brown Gray-vy. dk.

Top left • Stitch Count: 82 x 137

The Goose
that laid the
golden egg

The Goose that Laid the Golden Egg

Bottom left

120

Bottom right

121

The Wind and the Sun were arguing about which was the stronger when they saw a man walking down the road. The sun said, "Whichever one of us can cause that traveler to take off his coat is the stronger."

The Sun went behind a cloud as the Wind blew hard upon the man. The man felt the cold and held the coat tightly around his shoulders. Then the Sun came out and shone brightly. The man found the sunshine delightful, and removed his cloak to enjoy it.

"Warmth and persuasion are always more powerful than cold force," said the Sun.

The Wind and the Sun

The Wind and the Sun

SAMPLE

Stitched on Platinum Belfast Linen 32 over two threads, the finished design size is 6¾" x 9". The fabric was cut 13" x 15". Frame as desired.

Other Fabrics	Finished Design
Aida 11	9⅞" x 13"
Aida 14	7¾" x 10¼"
Aida 18	6" x 8"
Hardanger 22	5" x 6½"

Anchor		DMC (used for sample)	

Step 1: Cross-stitch (2 strands)

892		3770	Peach Pecan-vy. lt.
891		676	Old Gold-lt.
337		3778	Terra Cotta
870		3042	Antique Violet-lt.
872		3740	Antique Violet-dk.
928		598	Turquoise-lt.
920		932	Antique Blue-lt.
921		931	Antique Blue-med.
900		928	Slate Green-lt.
905		3781	Mocha Brown-dk.
236		3799	Pewter Gray-vy. dk.

Step 2: Backstitch (1 strand)

236		3799	Pewter Gray-vy. dk.

Top left • Stitch Count: 109 x 143

The Wind and the Sun

A Wolf in Sheep's Clothing

BEWARE OF A W

THAT IS

Once there was an old wolf who liked to eat sheep. Day after day he watched them, but he could not catch any because of the diligent shepherd. One day he found a sheep's skin. He put it on his back and went to graze with the sheep. They were not afraid of him because he looked like them. He crept up beside a fat lamb and quickly gobbled him up.

"So beware of a wolf who is all white and woolish. He's liable to eat a lamb that is foolish!"

A Wolf in Sheep's Clothing

SAMPLE
Stitched on Amaretto Murano 30
over two threads, the finished design size is
4⅞" x 7⅛". The fabric was cut 11" x 13".
Frame as desired.

Other Fabrics	Finished Design
Aida 11	7⅛" x 10⅜"
Aida 14	5⅝" x 8⅛"
Aida 18	4⅜" x 6⅜"
Hardanger 22	3½" x 5⅛"

Anchor			DMC	(used for sample)

Step 1: Cross-stitch (2 strands)

Anchor			DMC	Color
926				Ecru
366			951	Peach Pecan-lt.
326			720	Orange Spice-dk.
13			347	Salmon-vy. dk.
95			554	Violet-lt.
101			327	Antique Violet-vy. dk.
121			793	Cornflower Blue-med.
941			791	Cornflower Blue-vy. dk.
161			3760	Wedgewood-med.
242			989	Forest Green
246			319	Pistachio Green-vy. dk.
381			838	Beige Brown-vy. dk.
236			3799	Pewter Gray-vy. dk.
403			310	Black

Step 2: Backstitch (1 strand)

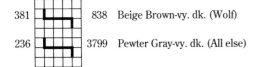

381		838	Beige Brown-vy. dk. (Wolf)
236		3799	Pewter Gray-vy. dk. (All else)

Top • Stitch Count: 78 x 114

The Tortoise and the Hare

The Tortoise challenged the Hare to a race to a tree by the river. The Hare laughed, and as the race began, he ran down the road so quickly that he could no longer see the Tortoise.

There is no need for me to run so fast," he thought. "I will lie in this soft grass and rest for a while." When the Hare awoke, he ran to the tree down by the river, expecting to win the race, but the Tortoise was there waiting for him. Slow and steady wins the race.

THE
TORTOISE
AND THE
HARE

The Tortoise and the Hare

SAMPLE
Stitched on Antique Blue Linen 32 over two threads, the finished design size is 6¼" x 3¾". The fabric was cut 12" x 10". Frame as desired.

Other Fabrics	Finished Design
Aida 11	9⅛" x 5⅜"
Aida 14	7⅛" x 4¼"
Aida 18	5½" x 3¼"
Hardanger 22	4½" x 2⅝"

Anchor			DMC (used for sample)

Step 1: Cross-stitch (2 strands)

926			Ecru
896			3722 Shell Pink
897			221 Shell Pink-vy. dk.
167			3766 Peacock Blue-lt.
870			3042 Antique Violet-lt.
101			327 Antique Violet-vy. dk.
862			520 Fern Green-dk.
392			642 Beige Gray-dk.
236			3799 Pewter Gray-vy. dk.

Step 2: Backstitch (1 strand)

236		3799 Pewter Gray-vy. dk.

Left • Stitch Count: 101 x 59

134

STEADY

s the race

The country mouse and the City mouse

the difference betw
country life and a co

The Country Mouse

A City Mouse went to visit his cousin in the country. The Country Mouse welcomed him to his home, but all he had to offer were corn and grains stored under some dried leaves. The City Mouse said, "Come with me and I will show you how to live."

The two mice set off for town and arrived at the City Mouse's home. They feasted on the remains of jellies and cakes in the dining room. Suddenly, they were chased from the room by a large barking dog. "Better corn and grains in peace than jellies and cakes in fear," cried the Country Mouse as he ran out the door to return to his home in the country.

and City Mouse

The Country Mouse and City Mouse

SAMPLE
Stitched on White Cashel Linen 28
over two threads, the finished design size is
6⅞" x 10⅝". The fabric was cut 13" x 17".
Frame as desired.

Other Fabrics	Finished Design
Aida 11	8⅞" x 13½"
Aida 14	6⅞" x 10⅝"
Aida 18	5⅜" x 8¼"
Hardanger 22	4⅜" x 6¾"

Top left • Stitch Count: 97 x 149

Anchor   **DMC (used for sample)**

Step 1: Cross-stitch (2 strands)

Anchor			DMC	
293	○	◺	727	Topaz-vy. lt.
306	▢		725	Topaz
890	▲		729	Old Gold-med.
8	▪	◿	353	Peach
10	❙	◿	3712	Salmon-med.
13	●	◿	347	Salmon-vy. dk.
95	⦂		554	Violet-lt.
98	❙		553	Violet-med.
117	▪	◿	3747	Blue Violet-vy. lt.
160	∴	◿	3761	Sky Blue-lt.
168	◎		518	Wedgewood-lt.
206	△		955	Nile Green-lt.

Anchor			DMC	
210	✕	◺	562	Jade-med.
363	−	◿	436	Tan
370	◹	◿	434	Brown-lt.
900	▪	◿	3024	Brown Gray-vy. lt.
8581	✕	◿	3022	Brown Gray-med.
236		◾	3799	Pewter Gray-vy. dk.

Step 2: Backstitch (1 strand)

236	⌐	3799	Pewter Gray-vy. dk.

Step 3: French Knot (1 strand)

236	●	3799	Pewter Gray-vy. dk.

Top right

The Country Mouse and City Mouse

Center left

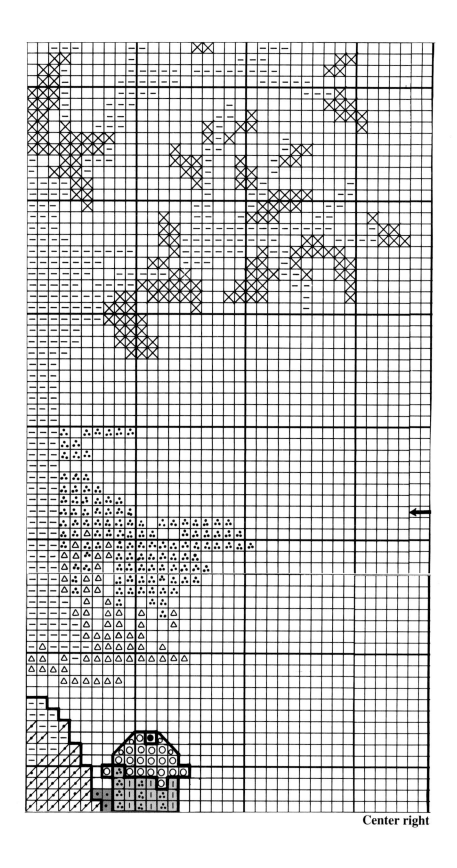

Center right

The Country Mouse and City Mouse

the difference betw

country life and a cour

xt a
tly life.

143

Androcles was a poor farmer searching for a fertile area. As he walked, he came upon a lion with a long, sharp thorn in its paw. Androcles pulled the thorn from the lion's paw and continued walking.

The next day, the King's soldiers captured Androcles, thinking him an enemy from another country. Androcles was placed in an arena, and a hungry lion was released from his cage. The lion was the same one that Androcles had earlier helped. The lion recognized him as a friend and licked his hands and face.

Androcles and the Lion

Androcles and the Lion

SAMPLE

Stitched on Confederate Gray Belfast
Linen 32 over two threads, the finished design
size is 6½" x 5¼". The fabric was cut
13" x 12". Frame as desired.

Other Fabrics	Finished Design
Aida 11	9½" x 7⅝"
Aida 14	7⅜" x 6"
Aida 18	5¾" x 4⅝"
Hardanger 22	4¾" x 3⅞"

Anchor   DMC (used for sample)

Step 1: Cross-stitch (2 strands)

99			552	Violet-dk.
885			739	Tan-ultra vy. lt.
362			437	Tan-lt.
341			919	Red Copper
378			841	Beige Brown-lt.
380			839	Beige Brown-dk.
381			838	Beige Brown-vy. dk.

Step 2: Backstitch (1 strand)

| 381 | | 838 | Beige Brown-vy. dk. |

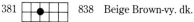

Step 3: French Knot (1 strand)

| 381 | | 838 | Beige Brown-vy. dk. |

Top left • Stitch Count: 104 x 84

147

Androcles and the Lion

Bottom left

148

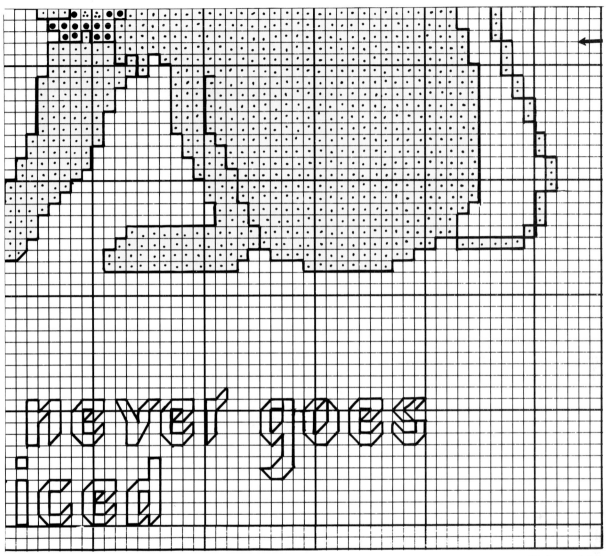

Bottom right

The Fisherman and

His Wife

A fisherman and his wife lived in a little house beside a river. One day the fish did not bite. He knew that if he did not catch a fish, he and his wife would have nothing to eat.

At last he caught one small fish. As he removed the hook the fish said, "I am so small, I will not make a very big dinner. Throw me back into the water, and when I get bigger, I will make a fine meal."

The fisherman put the fish into his basket and walked back towards his home.

"You may be small," he said, "but a small fish is better than no fish at all."

The Fisherman and His Wife

SAMPLE

Stitched on Antique White Murano 30 over two threads, the finished design size is 9⅜" x 8⅞". The fabric was cut 16" x 15". Frame as desired.

Other Fabrics	Finished Design
Aida 11	12¾" x 12⅛"
Aida 14	10" x 9½"
Aida 18	7¾" x 7⅜"
Hardanger 22	6⅜" x 6"

Anchor			DMC	(used for sample)
Step 1:	Cross-stitch (2 strands)			
271			3713	Salmon-vy. lt.
8			761	Salmon-lt.
9			760	Salmon
10			3712	Salmon-med.
158			3756	Baby Blue-ultra vy. lt.
157			828	Blue-ultra vy. lt.
154			775	Baby Blue-vy. lt.
159			827	Blue-vy. lt.
160			3325	Baby Blue-lt.
145			334	Baby Blue-med.
161			826	Blue-med.
185			964	Seagreen-lt.
186			959	Seagreen-med.
187			958	Seagreen-dk.
256			704	Chartreuse-bright

Top left • Stitch Count: 140 x 133

239			702	Kelly Green
229			700	Christmas Green-bright
264			472	Avocado Green-ultra lt.
266			471	Avocado Green-vy. lt.
267			469	Avocado Green
265			3348	Yellow Green-lt.
817			3347	Yellow Green-med.
268			3345	Hunter Green-dk.

269			936	Avocado Green-vy. dk.
388			3033	Mocha Brown-vy. lt.
903			3032	Mocha Brown-med.
309			435	Brown-vy. lt.
371			433	Brown-med.
397			762	Pearl Gray-vy. lt.
398			415	Pearl Gray
400			414	Steel Gray-dk.

| 403 | | | 310 | Black |

Step 2: Long stitch (1 strand)

| 403 | | 310 | Black |

Step 3: Backstitch (1 strand)

| 403 | | 310 | Black |

153

The Fisherman and His Wife

Bottom left

Bottom right

The Leopard and the Fox

A leopard sat in a tree, admiring his beautiful, spotted coat. "I am certainly the finest animal in the forest," he said to himself. A fox passing by overheard him.

"It is too bad you cannot change your spots," he said to the leopard.

The leopard was surprised. "If you had a coat as beautiful, perhaps you would not be jealous," he said.

The fox replied, "I have no spots or glossy finish, but I am content to be the most clever animal in the forest."

There is more to a person than meets the eye.

The Leopard and the Fox

SAMPLE

Stitched on Ivory Murano 30 over two threads, the finished design size is 10⅝" x 10". The fabric was cut 17" x 16". Frame as desired.

Other Fabrics	Finished Design
Aida 11	14½" x 13¾"
Aida 14	11⅜" x 10¾"
Aida 18	8⅞" x 8⅜"
Hardanger 22	7¼" x 6⅞"

Anchor	DMC (used for sample)	
Step 1: Cross-stitch (2 strands)		
1		White
293	727	Topaz-vy. lt.
295	726	Topaz-lt.
306	725	Topaz
303	742	Tangerine-lt.

Anchor	DMC	
307	783	Christmas Gold
309	781	Topaz-dk.
49	963	Wild Rose-vy. lt.
74	3354	Dusty Rose-vy. lt.
75	3733	Dusty Rose-lt.
76	3731	Dusty Rose-med.
158	775	Baby Blue-vy. lt.
159	3325	Baby Blue-lt.
160	813	Blue-lt.
145	334	Baby Blue-med.
161	826	Blue-med.
162	825	Blue-dk.
164	824	Blue-vy. dk.
149	311	Navy Blue-med.
264	472	Avocado Green-ultra lt.
265	471	Avocado Green-vy. lt.
266	470	Avocado Green-lt.

Anchor	DMC	
267	469	Avocado Green
238	703	Chartreuse
239	702	Kelly Green
227	701	Christmas Green-lt.
255	907	Parrot Green-lt.
256	906	Parrot Green-med.
258	904	Parrot Green-vy. dk.
204	912	Emerald Green-lt.
205	911	Emerald Green-med.
228	910	Emerald Green-dk.
229	909	Emerald Green-vy. dk.
244	987	Forest Green-dk.
879	890	Pistachio Green-ultra dk.
887	372	Mustard-lt.
888	371	Mustard
889	370	Mustard-med.

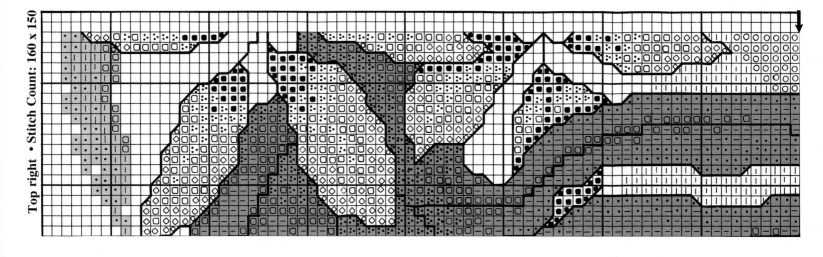

Top right • Stitch Count: 160 x 150

362	437	Tan-lt.
363	436	Tan
309	435	Brown-vy. lt.
370	434	Brown-lt.
376	842	Beige Brown-vy. lt.
378	841	Beige Brown-lt.
379	840	Beige Brown-med.
380	839	Beige Brown-dk.
387	822	Beige Gray-lt.
397	762	Pearl Gray-vy. lt.
399	318	Steel Gray-lt.
400	317	Pewter Gray
401	413	Pewter Gray-dk.
403	310	Black

Step 2: Backstitch (1 strand)

| 403 | 310 | Black |

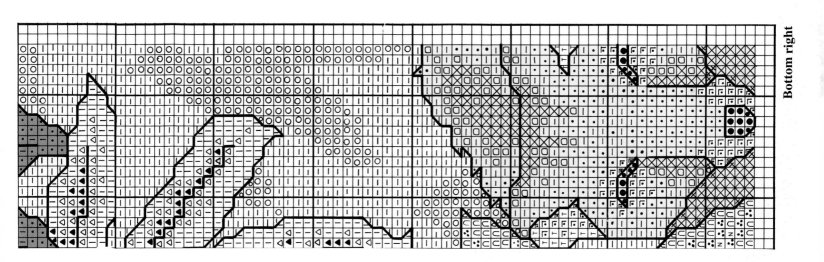

Bottom right

159

Top center

161

The Leopard and the Fox

Top left

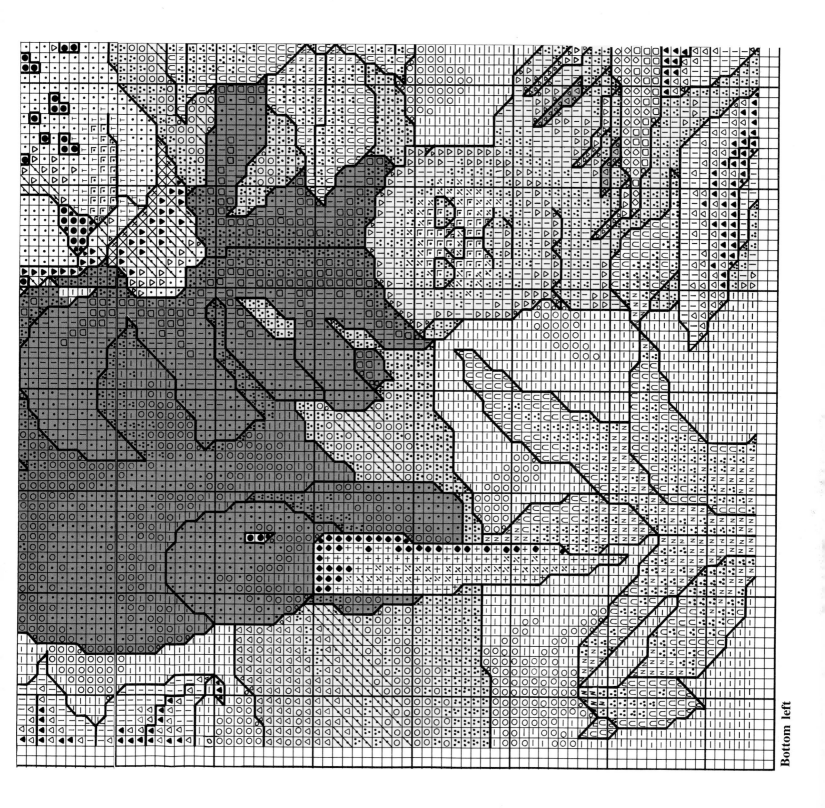

General Instructions for Cross-Stitch

Easy Reference Features

The SAMPLE paragraphs describe the design pieces in each photograph. They also contain any special instructions for stitching or for cutting fabric. When applicable, finished design sizes are also given for other fabrics you may wish to use.

On the graphs, each square containing a symbol represents one cross-stitch and corresponds to a specific thread color as indicated on the color code. The stitch count printed with a graph lists first the width, then the length of the design.

The color codes identify thread by color, number, and brand. The symbols correspond to the symbols on the graphs. The color codes also indicate the kinds of stitches and number of floss strands to use.

Fabrics

Cut the fabric at least 3" larger on all sides than the design size or cut it the size specified in the SAMPLE information. A 3" margin is the minimum amount of fabric required to ensure plenty of space for matting, framing, and other finishing techniques for your stitched piece. To keep fabric from fraying, whipstitch or machine-zigzag the raw edges, or apply liquid ravel preventer and allow to dry. Using a stretcher bar frame or a hoop keeps fabric from wrinkling, ensuring uniform stitches.

Centering the Design

Unless otherwise indicated in the directions, the design should be centered on the fabric. Fold fabric in half horizontally, then vertically. Place a pin in the point of the fold to mark the center. Locate the center of the design on the graph by following the paths of the vertical and horizontal arrows printed on the edges of each graph to their intersection. Begin stitching at the center of the graph and fabric.

Needles

A blunt tapestry needle, size 24 or 26, will slip easily through fabric holes without piercing fabric threads. Never leave a needle in the design area of the work; it may leave rust or a permanent impression on the fabric.

Stitching

Cut thread into 18" lengths; longer pieces tend to twist and knot. Run floss over a damp sponge to straighten. Separate the strands, then use the number of strands indicated in the color code. Thread should lie flat; if it begins to twist, suspend the needle and allow it to unwind.

Secure the thread by inserting the needle up from the underside of the fabric at the starting point. Hold 1" of thread behind the fabric and stitch over it with the first few stitches. Another method for securing thread is the waste knot. Knot the thread and bring the needle down through the fabric about 1" from where first stitch will be. Work several stitches over the thread to secure. Cut off the knot later. To finish thread, run it under several stitches on the back of the work.

To carry thread, weave it under previously worked stitches on the back of the design. Do not carry thread across fabric that is not or will not be stitched. Loose threads, especially dark ones, will show through.

Beadwork

Cross-stitch all non-beaded areas of design before doing any beadwork. Apply each bead in the same manner as a cross-stitch (see Diagram on opposite page): stitch from lower left to upper right, passing floss through bead; bring needle up again at lower right, pass through bead again, and insert at upper left. When working in rows, first make all left-to-right diagonal stitches in the row, then return to secure beads with the right-to-left diagonal stitches.

Cleaning Completed Work

Soak finished design piece in cold water with mild soap for 5-10 minutes; rinse. Roll in a towel to remove excess water; do not wring. Place face down on a dry towel and iron on a warm setting until dry.

Stitches Used

Cross-Stitch and Half Stitch

Back Stitch

Beading

French Knot

General Instructions for Pillows

Bias Strips

Cut fabric square in half diagonally (along the bias). Beginning at one 45-degree corner, fold fabric several times (see Diagrams below), aligning bias edge, until opposite corner is met. Cut strips of required width for binding or piping, parallel to bias edge. For ¼" piping, cut strips at least 1" wide; for ⅜" piping, at least 1¼"-wide strips are required. Join strip ends along straight grain to make a longer strip of required length.

Mitering Corners

After pillow center is completed, stitch on any border strips, beginning and ending at the adjacent seam allowances. Backstitch. Fold two overlapping border strips or fabric corners together at a 45-degree angle, as shown in Diagram. Mark both sides; pin and then sew on marked line. Trim seam allowance to ¼". Repeat for all four corners.

Corded Piping or Ruffles

To make piping, encase a length of cord in a pieced bias strip and stitch as closely as possible, using a zipper foot. To attach piping or ruffles, pin around right side of pillow front, beginning at center of one edge, so that stitching line of piping or ruffle lies on seam line and flat/apron edge of piping is inside seam allowance. Stitch up to seam allowance of adjacent edge: Pivot with needle in fabric at corner. Clip flat/apron edge of piping up to seam line. Continue stitching next edge.

To finish ends of ruffle (if not already joined), leave about 1" free when starting place is reached, make neat seam across ruffle ends, finish stitching ruffle to pillow.

To finish ends of piping, remove 1" of stitching at each end of bias strip. Fold under ¼" of fabric at one strip end; lap raw end over folded end. Trim cord so ends butt. Whipstitch piping ends together and refold bias strip. Finish stitching to pillow.

Finishing

Once the front of the pillow has been completed, place it on top of the backing, right sides facing together. Sew the two pieces together, leaving a 3"-4" opening for turning and stuffing in one side. Turn pillow right side out through the opening; stuff, then slipstitch the opening closed.

Suppliers

Fabric

Zweigart/Joan Toggitt Ltd.
Weston Canal Plaza
2 Riverview Drive
Somerset, NJ 08873
(908) 271-1949

Antique White Belfast Linen 32
Confederate Gray Belfast Linen 32
Cream Belfast Linen 32
Light Mocha Belfast Linen 32
Platinum Belfast Linen 32
Sand Belfast Linen 32
White Belfast Linen 32
Amaretto Murano 30
Antique White Murano 30
Ash Rose Murano 30
Cream Murano 30
Ivory Murano 30
Pewter Murano 30
White Murano 30
White Cashel Linen 28

Wichelt Imports, Inc.
RR1
Stoddard, WI 54658
(608) 788-4600

Antique Blue Linen 32
Delicate Teal Jobelan 28

Floss and Beads

Floss
The DMC Corporation
Contact:
American Needlewoman
(800) 433-2231
Herrschner's
(800) 441-0838

Mill Hill Beads
Gay Bowles Sales, Inc.
P.O. Box 1060
Janesville, WI 53547
(608) 754-9466

032HL Balger Pearl Blending Filament
017HL Balger Blending Filament
Kreinik Mfg. Co, Inc.
P..O. Box 1966
Parkersburg, WV 26101
(800) 537-2166

Kits and Accessories

Polyester stuffing
Fleece
Fairfield Processing Corp.
P.O. Box 1157
Danbury, CT 06813-1157
(800) 243-0989

#912 Box with insert top
Freeman & Co.
416 Julian Avenue
Thomasville, NC 27360
(910) 476-4936

Clock
Sudbury House
Box 895
Old Lyme, CT 06371
(203) 739-6951

Index

All of us at Meredith® Press are dedicated to offering you, our customer, the best books we can create. We are particularly concerned that all of our instructions for making projects are clear and accurate. Please address your correspondence to Customer Service, Meredith® Press, 150 East 52nd Street, New York, NY 10022.

If you would like to order additional copies of any of our books, call 1-800-678-8091 or check with your local bookstore.